Lifting Waits

A Collection of Poems

Patricia M. Robertson

Copyright © 2020 by Patricia M. Robertson.

ISBN-978-1-6455-0821-2

All rights reserved. No part of this book may be reproduced or transmitted in any form or by any means, electronic or mechanical, including photocopying, recording, or by any information storage and retrieval system, without permission in writing from the copyright owner.

The views expressed in this work are solely those of the author and do not necessarily reflect the views of the publisher, and the publisher hereby disclaims any responsibility for them.

Matchstick Literary
1-888-306-8885
orders@matchliterary.com

Contents

Seaside Frolics 1
Rippling 2
School Lunches 3
Meetings 4
Searching 5
Roaming 6
Love and Death 7
No Ordinary Journey 8
Newborn 10
Transit Part One 11
Remembrance 12
The Purging of Love Lost 13
Prelude to a Storm 15
Magnetism 16
Tall Trees 17
Seek 18
The Journey of Love 19
Soul 20
The Wild Woman Calling 21
When I Grow Up 22
Rainbow Climbing 23
Reflections of the Soul 24
After the Wars 25
Bedtime Tale 26
The Lifting 27
The Fight 28

Staying Here	29
Letting Go	30
Soul Talk	31
Cleansing	32
The Tightrope	34
Changing Course	35
Tide and Time	36
Burning	37
Farewell in White Mist	38
Missing You	39
The Raging Fire	40
Waiting	41
Authors' Note	42

… A girl dressed in blue stands on a cliff. Her gown curdles round the swirling winds. Her tears fall like raindrops in a storm. Clouds lift her from rocky shores and cradle her wounded soul …

— *Patricia M. Robertson*

This book is dedicated to Dr Gregor Schutz, whose support, guidance, care and commitment to me, helped me complete this book and my most important person on the planet, my father, Mr Alexander J. Robertson.

Seaside Frolics

Solutated signals signing summer has started.
Robust rogues running riot.
Tiring teenagers, toffee-tight T-shirts.
Queuing customers keeping quiet.

Policy persons perspiring, perplexed.
Seaside souls' slippery sweat.
Hankies hankering hollow heads.
Swift surf surging salty hair sets.

Jeans juggling Jupiter jazz.
Rock rolling razzmatazz.
Kiss, cuddle, cute, and kept.
Love lingers, longing to let.

Animated animals, anonymous, alive.
Whistling wonders, wallowing wives.
Belching bellies, browny burnt.
Those who were scorched and those who weren't.
And the sun shone, and everyone yawned.

Rippling

Pools of clear visions rippling.
A distant village in darkness.
Rays, yellow like egg yolk, radiate
from street lamps.
Blue waters, with a cool meringue,
bubble over and sizzle on
a tepid sand at midnight.
A strong smell of fish.
A girl dressed in blue stands on a cliff.
Her gown curdles round the swirling winds.
Her tears fall like raindrops in a storm.
Clouds lift her from rocky shores
and cradle her wounded soul.
Her blonde hair blankets a threatening sky
as she leaves her townstead, where memories lie.
Her soul is a misted length of chiffon,
which wraps itself around eternal pain
and aches as a forever wind, unsettled in its grave,
just wishes to be left alone to gather dust,
ferment with age.
When one day a bloom of youth
will pick her up in fragile fingers
and blow away the scattered cobwebs.

School Lunches

Sixty thousand crimping chaps,
wandering down with pink flowery hats,
12:20 p.m. nailed to the door.
Gushing, gaping mouths hit elasticated door,
filing like soldiers.

12:45 p.m. glance over empty tables,
grand sweep of empty plates labelled.
Out to Australia and lands far away,
out to the grass ready for play.

They love our money in their sweaty palms.
Never ask questions.
"Haven't I seen you right down the line?"
"I'm in your maths class, XTL9."

12:46 p.m. second time round.
Licking lips smack.
Big, clompy boots clickety-clack,
hit undernourished souls and lunches.

Meetings

Mild debates on federate grounds,
stinking collars.
Topic discussions in curved air.
Backstreet crawlers wanting the dazzle.
"Smile for the camera, the one with the specs."
Gripping cigars—psychotics.

Crouched on support, folding his legs.
Collars and ties hanging vertical,
like pegs.
Tinted his head to a silvery brown.
The flaw of society.
The talk of the town.

Searching

I look for your smile in the maddening crowd;
the look on your face fixed firmly on my mind.
I sometimes ache for your touch,
but I know you are not mine.

Why does this love torture my brain?
I meditate to control the pain.
I will survive alone as I have always done,
to be without you as I have always been.

Roaming

I listen to a voice
that is not my own.
I swell on the high seas
that are not my home.
So I roam, and I roam
through the wars and the peace.
I'm alone on the road.
I talk to a person
about my fear and the cold.
I'm a soul with a shield.
Don't kill it as it yields.
I have to go alone
until I find the fields
in my spirit that is my home.

Love and Death

She wonders about her purpose
when life right now ain't no circus.
He walked away one June warm day.
"Heaven took him without my say," she yelled.
"Why? Who gave the order and signed?"
No answer came; she had no say
on the things that are divine.
She need only remember
they were souls caught by time,
and the fate of humanity
seems on the decline.
Her spirit walks now on empty land.
Her body rolls down yellow sand,
closer than ever to the sea.
The force of nature resurrects me.
Green leaves shuffle in the wind.
People, like ants, get tempted and sin.
Then his spirit breathes gently in her ear;
she knows that often he follows her near.
These are the things that she has to tell.
It keeps her out of a living hell.
She's been there before, and she ain't going back.
This girl's out searching for a different track.

No Ordinary Journey

Down an unfamiliar street,
there's a tiredness in her walk.
If there's an end to this eternal path,
she can't see it, and it doesn't stop.
"I don't know where the good times are,"
she says while walking through the dark.
Many daggers have pierced her fragile heart.
She thought this pain made her stand apart.
Not in some superior way, for better or for worse,
than the average traveller with no money in her purse.
But she is alone with it all now.
There's no one to call down the hall.
"It's meant to be this way,"
a voice whispers in her ear.
"It's meant to hurt."
"But what about the fear?" she asks.
"Am I too dangerous to be near?"
Vulnerable through the years.
Back on the street that never ends,
a familiar friend that makes her mad and sad.
Where there's no one there to tell.
No soulful friend on this journey alone.
Tiredness in her bones,
wearing the past like a coat.
In her castle, surrounded by a moat,
armoured on with shining steel.
"It's got to be the time to start to heal."

She's so determined not to feel.
Looking out from her spiral tower,
it's now time to find her power.
She looks up to the sky to find the light,
the light that resides inside her.
The light she fights for with all her might,
which was stolen by the demons
who haunt her in the night.
Just waiting for her to crash,
so they can have another bash.
She keeps right on walking on this street.
It's her unfamiliar journey now.
"She's not to kill it," she hears.
"Because the girl has got spirit."

Newborn

Resurrected from a darkened slumber,
painted pastel beginnings etch their paths
over timid shades of light.
A palette of dancing pink and blue
wash over a sterile landscape,
spreading a blanket of expectation;
teasing, tickling, curling around
the threaded, woven pastures
still damp with afterbirth.
Whispering leaves draped on oaken branches
chatter anxiously as a scented breeze
caresses fragile newcomers.
Scattered in batches of frosting green and
lemon yellow.
A watery egg yolk light spills over
rocky crevices where sleeping young
lie warm and protected.
Waiting for mother.
Hanging cobwebs sprinkled with tears
of bitter yesterdays glisten.
Droplets form translucent clusters
of diamonds and sapphires.
A richness transient with the
warming breath of milder tomorrows.

Transit Part One

I'm searching for my voice.
Have you heard it?
Do you know where I can find it?
Is it still in the pit
where I lost it?

When the darkness consumed it
and coloured it with the night.
Cruel and crude,
sick and bestial and arid.
Am I being rude?

The voice that once guided me
died in a pit made up of my own horror,
depression, dread, and destructiveness.
Where my voice went.
In the dark pit where I lost it.

Remembrance

He's still in my head,
even when I go to bed.
Out of my dreams at last.
So far back into the past.
Was there love?
Was I strong?
What went wrong?
Lessons learned.
Another song.
They say out of
chaos comes peace.
Out of this conflict
I will be released.

The Purging of Love Lost

Don't think you can walk back
on any attack.
Get down on your knees,
and say, "Please," with ease.
Then we'll be on equal ground,
and we'll get back to
what we found.
But this time,
it'll be a different round.

Divine intervention makes the rules.
We just carry them out.
Scream and shout.
Get drunk and make out.
Now, no more will this ever be.
I'm a swimmer now on my
emotional sea.

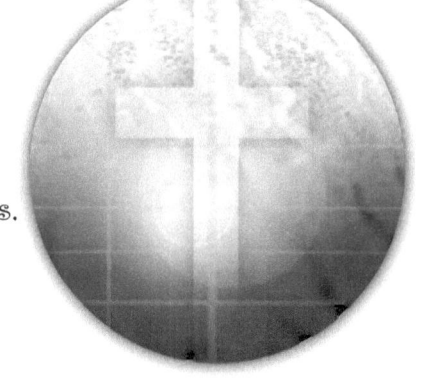

So don't think you
can make it without
ever consulting me.
Keep your mind in your head
and your dick in the sink.
It might just give you
enough time to think.
Don't ever cry on my shoulder
before you bite.

It'll just end in tears
and another fight.
We move in different ways;
right or wrong, who says?

Take the position of judge
if that's your way,
but don't be surprised
if God's with me
the first time you pray.
What makes me think
I have that claim?
Because I'm no longer
in that dog game of blame.

It's such a shame to
shame the lame,
but you've got to have
someone to blame.
So it's all the same.
Just a game.
I'm tired of hunting.
Let me have the sleep I'm wanting.
Allow the peace to flow on
into our relationship of past and sin.
To be forgotten in the brain,
like there are no remains.
Cremated to the wind
because you judge my sins.

Because you always have to win.

Prelude to a Storm

A dark and icy death
at 1 a.m. twenty-first of April,
when risen from the murky depth,
did souls gather on the dangerous cliff.
The old caretaker wets his whiskers with a spirit relief.
The factory sign swings in the evening heat.
Distant crooner hums a mellow beat.
Offshore, a small trawler sways off to sleep.
The weather report brings rain twelve minutes
after one, and the lady on the radio says,
"Keep me turned on."
The fog bank gathers on the dark horizon,
and the couple on the seashore gaze into the
watery sweep of blue froth and whisper.

Magnetism

He had the sophistication.
It crumbled her to dust.
She was marshmallow in his hands.
He, the cream on the top of the milk.
She licked her smooth lips with her tongue
and gazed at his body with hungry eyes.

He was totally unattainable.
She stalked him like a panther.
Insatiable, she followed his movements.
If she breathed heavily enough,
he would feel it on the back of his neck.
But she held back because he was the dangerous one.

His passion drew blood from her heart.
She was his slave.
"Tea?" he asked with the prowess of a prince.
"White and one," she replied.
"Music?"
"Bach."
"Sex?"
"Tea and chocolate cake if you've got any."

Tall Trees

The tree that grew the tallest
was fed to be the strongest.
All the little ones couldn't see
above that tallest tree.
Its branches cradled puffy clouds,
sheltering its trunk raw and thick.
Then one day man came long,
chopped it down, and made it
into wooden sticks.
Big, think trunk had no brains;
thought he could see it all
except the bastard that made him fall.
Bark scattered on bare plateau.
So the little ones could grow
all same size; big boy gone,
babes bark all day long.
Man lies waiting.

Seek

No foolish wanderings will I now do.
Through the streets I've searched
for a look or a sigh
or a smile.
Stand at the entrance;
that's what I'll now do.
When he's ready, he'll come,
and I won't ask why.

The sun will come out,
and the gates will slide.

We'll enter it together,
and I'll never have to hide.

No fear where there's love;
that's what I have learned.
My minds' voice tell me,
but we keep it quiet.
Standing at the entrance
with a watchful eye.

The Journey of Love

And in the very beginning, there was a dark force,
and it was the end of an era.
But she didn't know it at the time
because it was so dark in there.
And for a long time, there didn't seem
to be anyone there for her.
But she was on a fated journey.
If only she had known that,
then all the pain she had endured
would have made more sense to her.
She was still on the journey,
but now it was making sense.
She had to understand
why she had been through the pain.
In this lifetime, she had to learn to love herself.
And when she had done this,
the life she had dreamed of
and thought she had lost
would return to her in a different form.
This would be a good love.
At this point, she would move out
of her fate and on to her destiny.
And like a bud about to bloom,
her life would begin.

Soul

I touch like a dismembered body.
This touch which destroys.
Love will never come here.
I walk on water
which shifts and moves,
forever changing its form,
never settling on this deep and bitter soul.
Heated passion shrouded
in an icy cape of white silk,
waiting for the thaw,
when the ice will melt.
Seasons pass, but it doesn't change.
Winter comes yet again
on this passionate soul.

The Wild Woman Calling

When the time comes forth that she grows old,
she would be sure of stories never told.
The missed sweet kisses on her forehead,
pity in his eyes looking down on her in bed.
Wounds that only time could cure
and regret that, in the end, he was never sure.

Trapped in skin and societies whim,
she found a cave far away far from him.
Her spirit shattered, her soul deeply battered,
the Wild Woman called, and that's what mattered.
Each full moon the She woman called
through the bars in the prison with cream sterile walls.

The Wild Woman now is coming near
to empty out her past so that she can be clear
of her instincts, awareness, and perception,
and others' masks of deception and rejection.
Then to rise up through the mist on the mountains.
To sit in serenity near the waterfall fountains
with the love she had been robbed of and days of peace.
A smile on her face, and her spirit released.

When I Grow Up

And when I grow up,
I'll sail far away
to a place all alone.
With sea frothing bubbles,
I'll burst in the sun.
And make gold, sandy pictures.
Where people eat toast,
and drink cold cups of tea.
Making conversation,
most "confidentially".
And laugh in a pub,
throwing liquid down holes.
Who live in small boxes,
like captive moles.
Bringing home papers
with the latest events.
Moulded on sofas,
and glued to TV.
Making conversation
most "confidentially".
"Have a good day,
my tired honeybun?
How did it go?
Have any fun?"

Rainbow Climbing

There's a land beside a pot of gold.
You climb up a rainbow on a rope.
Hands get sweaty, the mind gets coloured;
you think of fathers, sisters,
brothers, and mothers.
It's the toughest journey you'll ever take.
It doesn't make true breathing in white mist.
All around, others think it is a tragic twist.

Walking the tightrope, no way back.
Take a spiritual sack with dreams in your soul
and a watchful eye on your biggest goal.
Don't say no but a silent yes.
Be placed on the crest as a welcome guest,
and bathe in the sun of all your tomorrows.
Wash away the tears of all your sorrows.

Be caressed in the love by something greater.
You're a survivor sent down by our Creator
to get over that rainbow that reflects in your eyes.
Never stop climbing, even in disguise,
Through the joy, conflict, love, and strife.
You are a reason for breathing.
You are a reason for life.

Reflections of the Soul

I was bruised and battered.
I didn't recognise myself.
I looked at my reflection in the window,
a woman once with potential wealth.

I scramble my way around suburban streets,
dark glasses on eyes that weep.
Long gone is the love to fill my soul.
Whether there is a future now, I do not know.

Why must it be that we suffer for love?
Why can't it come straight from the pleasures above?
When does it stop being incredibly hard
to find a soulmate who isn't scarred?

I've read that things come at the right time.
When will it be mine?
This isn't self-pity and doesn't lead me to drink.
All it makes me wonder is why I was born to think.

So much of me is healed in sleep.
The morning comes, and I don't greet the day.
With all my heart, I wish it was another way.
Another day.

After the Wars

There are the forgotten years,
all dead and crumbled to dust and rust.
We forget too quickly all the pain,
the hardest tears, and the bitter fears.
Wars still shed blood.
There are still the flood cracks in the earth.
The ships that never berth.
The sun we adorn is killing our young.

Begin to remember what we have to do
to survive after the feuds.
Where the lands part and empty.
There will be no more plenty.
Some survive to another language,
no peanut sandwich.

We cannot ignore the signs any longer.
Begin to get stronger in faith
and the power of peace.
It's the only solution before the revolution.
Otherwise, there will be fewer tomorrows,
fewer to sorrow.

Bedtime Tale

I've slept with darkness.
The cover of doom has
tucked me in at night.
Love has kissed my soul.
Death has made me fight.
Stripped away of those external things
and all the goodness that life's supposed to bring.

There are no more songs to play.
Never will I search the day.
Don't think this is all a dark tale.
I'd think you would think that,
especially if you are a male.
I've seen the sun come into my room.
The problem was it faded too soon.

The Lifting

Rippling clouds lifted her from rocky shores
and cradled her wounded soul.
Her long hair blanketed a threatening sky
as she left her homestead, where her memories lie.
Her soul was a misted length of chiffon
wrapped around eternal pain.

And ached as her forever spirit
was unsettled in its grave.
Just wishing to be left alone,
to gather dust and ferment with age.
Until one day when a bloom
of youth would pick her up
in fragile fingers
and blow away the scattered cobwebs.

The Fight

In the swollen belly of the night,
I drown in the mud that is my fight.
No hostages does this demon take.
He beckons me forward, and he's in weight,
telling me always that darkness is my fate.
Making me believe that my life's a mistake.

I listen alone as there is no one there.
Who would come to my hell, the place I'm ensnared.
It's fortunate for him that I no longer care.
There's a death going on, and nothing is fair.
Obstructed and ridiculed in every attempt
to get out of this nightmare until I'm awake.

Staying Here

A rainbow fades from the sky
just as I feel like saying, "Goodbye."
A reputation I can't mend,
with no love I wish to send.
All spent, every last cent,
on heaven's lent.
"Not so," says a voice in my ear.
Ever so close, "There's nothing to fear."

I'm not alone, I'm told.
So old I feel I just want to sleep.
A time to keep a future date.
Moving out of fate.
I have survived with my watchful eye
a spiritual spy
who won't let go.
"Why?" I want to know.

Letting Go

He's still in my head, even when I go to bed.
Out of my dreams at last,
so far back into the past.
Was there love?
Was I strong?
What went wrong?
Lessons learned, another song.
They say out of chaos comes the peace.
Out of this conflict, I will be released.

Soul Talk

You don't want me to cry.
Just don't tell me that's a lie,
and I'll try and say goodbye,
and I'll let it die.
Don't ask me why.

Tell me where's your paradise?
I used to see it in your eyes.
Why am I to let it go?
Do you really want to know?
Who knows, who knows?

I'm sitting on the edge of the world,
tearing my heart apart.
So they tell me that I'm smart.
What difference does it make
when we are so far apart?

Who's going to surf in your deep sea?
Is there someone other than me?
Don't jump in and out of my dreams.
I'm sitting down but cannot be
in between the love, loss and the angry.

Cleansing

Don't think you can just walk back after an attack.
Get down on your knees and say please.
Then I'll see you on an even ground,
and we may return to what we once found.
But this time it will be on a different round.
Divine intervention makes some rules.
We just carry them out—scream and shout,
get drunk, and make out.

No more will this ever be.
I'm now the swimmer in my emotional sea.
So don't think you can make it be
Without ever consulting me.
Keep your mind in your head
and your dick in the sink;
it might give you enough time to think.
Don't cry on your shoulder before you bite;
it'll just end up in tears and another fight.

We move in different ways.
Right or wrong, who says?
Take your position of judge if that's your way,
but don't be surprised if God's with me
the first time you pray.
What makes me think I can have that claim?
Because I'm no longer in the dog game of blame.

Let me have the sleep I'm wanting.
Allow the peace to flow on in
our relationship of past and sin.
To be forgotten in the brain,
like there are no remains
cremated to the wind.
Because you judge my sins.
Because you always have to win.

The Tightrope

The grey ground gravel's wet.
On slippery ground she's likely to sweat.
She's so used to falling and heaven calling.
It's almost like a bet; without the light, where would she be?
In some darkened land where love was banned,
and sex was an act of reproduction,
where she would switch on TV and get instruction.

She walks alone, looking for a place called home,
some kind of headlight, blinking to catch her eye
without her thinking.
If only to see the candle lit.
All over her body as its final hit.
Life never stays the same.
It takes a spark to light a flame,
to illuminate the lessons she has to learn.

Changing Course

A veil so transparent yet so densely made.
Even with time, it will never fade.
That and the man she dreams of through fire.
Love she desires who isn't a liar.
Now, for now she wants to sleep.
To have her freedom all to keep.

She thinks of the purest way to meet the light,
and the spirits who walk with her in the fight.
This injects some passion into her veins.
She's always letting go and is always on the change.
With the strengthening mind to bring her protection.
To leave the dark ones and their critical rejection.

She knows there's a summit that she can someday reach.
But will she be dead or living in her head
or loving in bed?

Tide and Time

There's a moon about to take over the sun of the day,
where shifting sands find a place they have to lay.
Never failing to surprise the oceans' undercurrent blues;
they know where they want to be when they choose.
And the life below the surface wonders at the days,
while the times of tomorrow wouldn't have it any other way.

Burning

Oh, the flesh, oh, the flesh of who she wants.
"Take your hands off him; he'll make you mad."
"Don't worry," says she, "I'm already bad."
The hellfire of want and heaven calling.
"You'll never get there," says the devil.
"You have no belonging."
The sordid pain of paying sex,
the detachment, the coldness, the boldness
that makes her spiral to the damnation.
"You'll never get out!" says the devil in exclamation.
He's on his way, she believes.
She tells the devil,
"I'm preparing a place in heavens' domain."
"You can't," says the devil. "I won't let you go."

Farewell in White Mist

She wanted to know where she had gone wrong.
Why she hadn't found the flame that isn't him.
He was her lover, deep in her heart,
but he left their place; they had to part.
But he couldn't leave; she wanted him so.
Yet one day she pushed him and said, "Now go."

White light all around her to the place where he had said no.
A place so far away she could never know.
She now knew she was no longer running the show.
He looked behind his shoulder as the guides took his hand.
He had to begin on a different ground; both souls who couldn't part,
crying and kissing each others' hearts scared to be apart.

One foot in, one foot out, he looked at her with tears in his eyes.
But she pushed him to the other world amid thankful, peaceful sighs
to one day return in disguise, to surprise her waiting heart.
And she would know him by the look in his eyes,
playful and ready for a future date.
Down on her knees she went and
prayed, "This time not fate."

Missing You
(Written for Christopher John Goldie 21/10/60–18/6/92)

Don't ever doubt my faith
in your eternal life.
It keeps my spirit gentle and light
when I bed down at night.
It's not easy down here;
you know that.
I've done what you've done.
There have been the knocks,
but I'm not in a box.
I love you so.
Too much to say there are no words to
express except in darkness,
when I'm on my knees.
So please,
keep coming into my space
for as long as you like,
until we get sweet again
in forever light.

The Raging Fire

Through the fire she walked.
Flames melted her skin,
until only her soul was left.
And that's all she wanted to leave.

She had finished with her body
and was relieved of her mind.
She was at peace,
finished with her troubled thoughts.
The fire raged on inside,
a burning mass too bright to look at.
Then a figure emerged.
It was her.

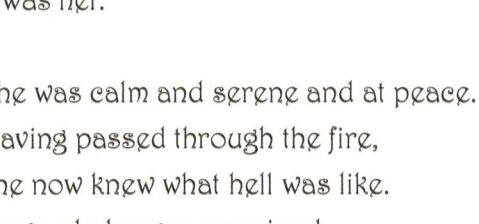

She was calm and serene and at peace.
Having passed through the fire,
she now knew what hell was like.
Now only heaven remained.

Waiting

No foolish wanderings will I now do.
Through the streets I've searched for a look or a sigh.
Stand at the entrance, that's what I'll now do.
When he's ready, he'll come, and I won't ask why.
The sun will come out, and the gates will slide.
We'll enter it together, and I'll never have to hide.
No fear where there's love, that's what I have learned.
My mind's voice tells me, but we keep it quiet.
Standing at the entrance with a watchful eye.

Authors' Note

I started writing before I was younger than ten years old, but I didn't like what I had written, so one night I made a bonfire in the garden and burned all of it. It wasn't until my family moved to Dundee, in 1978 in Scotland, to a home with an attic that I found my place to write.

Away from the family and in my own soul space, I found the source of my work. I never wrote to publish. I was seventeen years old. Writing was like being an artist, which I am, a pure soul release.

Relationships with men came at seventeen and I wrote to release the feeling and thoughts I couldn't tell them, any of them. Writing was a cathartic process.

In 1987 I moved to Melbourne from London where I had been working as a corporate show designer. I had a prolific career in film and multimedia design, (I have a B.A.(Hons) in design), but writing reached my depth. In the 1990's I studied Metaphysics under Rev Mario Schoenmaker at The Australian College of Metaphysics in Melbourne. I also studied for an Associate Diploma in Professional Writing at Holmesglen College in Melbourne, due to ill health I missed grammar in the certificate though was given several distinctions in short story writing and performance writing.

My only influence in my writing is in the Seaside Frolics which I wrote at seventeen years old. Dylan Thomas impressed me in the fact that he made up words to describe something, I liked that idea. The title for the book Lifting Waits comes from the idea that to come out of a dark place, a lifting of the the soul can take place, but sometimes the soul has to wait.

I have been published in theaustraliatimes.com.au, a magazine called Zadok and in The Best Poets Of The Twentieth Century in the year 2000 by Poetry.com.

My writing is a deep personal journey. I hope you enjoy my journey and thank you for the time you took to read this book.

Patricia M. Robertson